LOST!

Lisa Trumbauer

Raintree

www.raintreepublishers.co.uk

Visit our website to find out more information about **Raintree** books.

To order:
☎ Phone 44 (0) 1865 888112
🖹 Send a fax to 44 (0) 1865 314091
💻 Visit the Raintree bookshop at **www.raintreepublishers.co.uk** to browse our catalogue and order online.

First published in Great Britain by Raintree,
Halley Court, Jordan Hill, Oxford OX2 8EJ,
part of Harcourt Education.
Raintree is a registered trademark of Harcourt
Education Ltd.

Editorial: Louise Galpine and Catherine Veitch
Design: Michelle Lisseter and Bridge Creative Services
Illustrations: Bridge Creative Services
Picture Research: Hannah Taylor and Fiona Orbell
Production: Camilla Crask

Originated by Modern Age
Printed and bound in China by WKT Company
Limited

10-digit ISBN 1 406 20479 X (hardback)
13-digit ISBN 978 1 4062 0479 7
11 10 09 08 07
10 9 8 7 6 5 4 3 2 1

10-digit ISBN 1 406 20504 4 (paperback)
13-digit ISBN 978 1 4062 0504 6
11 10 09 08 07
10 9 8 7 6 5 4 3 2 1

**British Library Cataloguing in
Publication Data**
Trumbauer, Lisa, 1963-
Lost!. - (Fusion)
912'.014
A full catalogue record for this book is available from
the British Library.

Acknowledgements
The author and publisher are grateful to the
following for permission to reproduce copyright
material: Corbis p. **28** (Andrew Fox); Corbis p. **20**
(Conrad Zobel); Corbis pp. **4–5** (Lester Lefkowitz);
Corbis pp. **14–15** (Marvy!); Corbis/zefa pp. **22–23**
(Matthias Kulka); Getty Images/Amana Images pp.
18–19; Getty Images/Photodisc p. **7**; Getty
Images/Stone p. **8**, **16–17**; Getty Images/The Image
Bank p. **25**; Images France p. **11** (Graham Light);
Images France p. **27** (Ray Roberts); Pictures Colour
Library pp. **12–13** (Monica Wells).

Cover photograph with permission of Masterfile
(Bill Frymine).

Illustrations by Bridge Creative Services.

The publishers would like to thank Nancy Harris and
Daniel Block for their assistance in the preparation of
this book.

Every effort has been made to contact copyright
holders of any material reproduced in this book.
Any omissions will be rectified in subsequent
printings if notice is given to the publishers.

Disclaimer
All the Internet addresses (URLs) given in this book
were valid at the time of going to press. However,
due to the dynamic nature of the Internet, some
addresses may have changed, or sites may have
changed or ceased to exist since publication. While
the author and publishers regret any inconvenience
this may cause readers, no responsibility for any
such changes can be accepted by either the author
or the publishers.

It is recommended that adults supervise children on
the Internet.

Contents

Are you up for the challenge? 4

Task 1: Around the city 6

Task 2: All aboard! 10

Task 3: A smaller town 12

Task 4: Heading north 18

Task 5: Get out your compass 22

Well done! 26

Finding your way–the modern way 28

Glossary 30

Want to know more? 31

Index 32

Some words are printed in bold, **like this**. You can find out what they mean on page 30. You can also look in the box at the bottom of the page where they first appear.

Are you up for the challenge?

Earth is huge. It has wide oceans. It has large areas of land. They are called **continents**. It has **landforms** such as mountains and rivers. It has many cities and parks. Roads and rail lines connect these places. It is easy to get lost among the many landforms, cities, and roads! You need many tools to help you find your way.

Your challenge

Find your way from one point on Earth to another. You will begin in a huge, busy city. You will then be given step-by-step instructions. They will lead you to a smaller town. At the end of your trip, you will find an amazing building.

There is a catch. You cannot use any modern tools. You will just have a few maps, a ruler, and a **compass**. A compass is a tool that helps you find directions. It helps you find north, south, east, and west. You will have your own brainpower, too.

4

compass   tool to help you find the directions north, south, east, and west
continent   one of the seven largest pieces of land on Earth
landform   feature of the land such as a mountain, river, or beach

▼ From above you can see where things are. From land level, though, things are not as clear!

So, are you up for the challenge? Then let's get going!

Task 1: Around the city

> Find out where you are.

Where are you? Here are some clues to help you:

- **Clue 1:** Look at the tall building to the right.
  Do you know it?

- **Clue 2:** Important city buildings are usually named on
  a map. Can you find this tall building on the map below?

You are at the Eiffel Tower! You are in Paris! Paris is the
capital city of France. France is a country in Europe. Paris
has many streets and bridges. It has many important
buildings. It is very easy to get lost in a big city such as this.

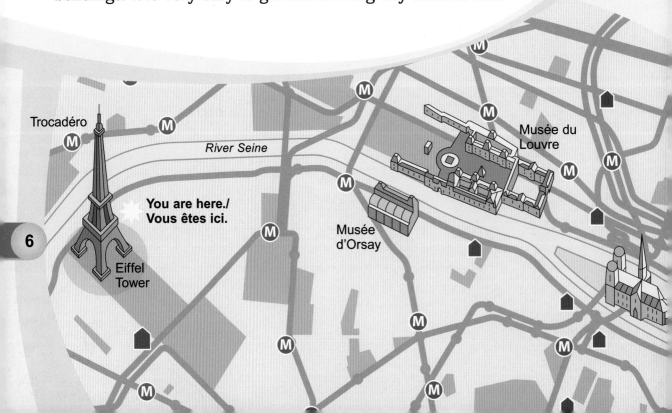

◀ Most cities have special buildings. This tower is not found anywhere else in the world. It is the Eiffel Tower. If you see the Eiffel Tower, you know you are in the city of Paris.

◀ Tourists are travellers. They visit places they have not been to before. A map such as this one helps tourists learn where things are in a new place.

Where will you go in Paris?

Going underground

Use your map to find a metro station.

You need to find the nearest **metro** station. A metro train runs under the ground in Paris. These trains are also known as tube trains.

All maps have a **map key**. The map key explains what the picture **symbols** on the map mean. The symbols on the map are small pictures or letters. Can you see the symbol for a metro station near the Eiffel Tower? It is an Ⓜ. Go to the metro station called *Trocadéro*.

Trocadéro Ⓜ

Key

Ⓜ tube/metro station ▬▬▬▬ road

🏠 museum ▦▦▦ park

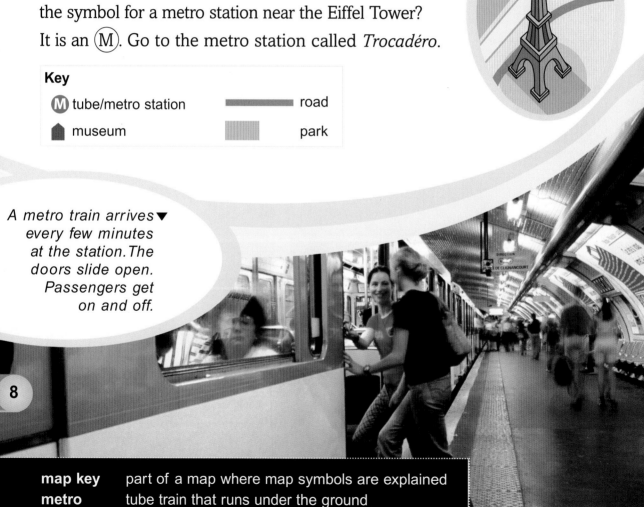

A metro train arrives ▼ *every few minutes at the station. The doors slide open. Passengers get on and off.*

8

map key   part of a map where map symbols are explained
metro   tube train that runs under the ground
metro line   path that a metro train follows
symbol   picture that stands for something else

Metro stations have maps, too. The maps show the different **metro lines**. A metro line is the path that certain metro trains always follow. Each coloured line on the metro map is a different metro line.

Your next stop is the north Paris train station. It is called *Gare du Nord*. Which colour metro lines must you take to get there?

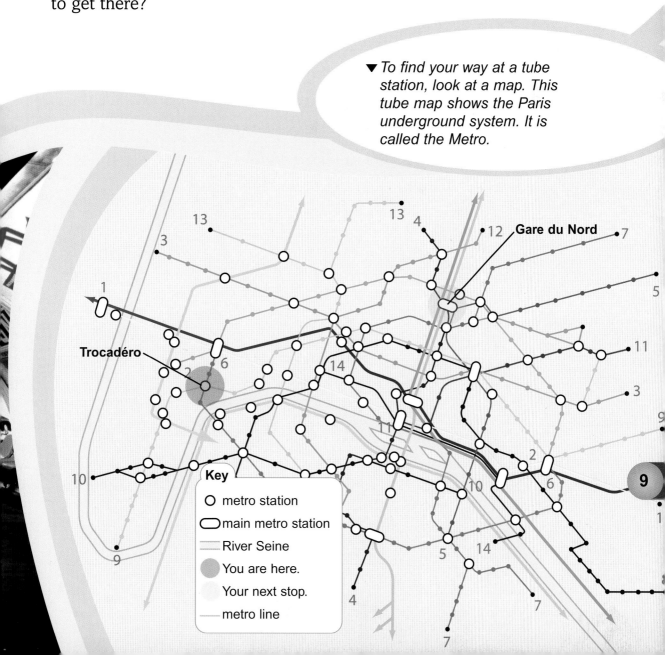

▼ *To find your way at a tube station, look at a map. This tube map shows the Paris underground system. It is called the Metro.*

Key

○ metro station

⬭ main metro station

River Seine

You are here.

Your next stop.

metro line

Task 2: All aboard!

Now, you need to catch another train to Calais.

Your **metro** train drops you off. You are at *Gare du Nord* station. Here, the trains run above ground from this station.

Look for a big board in the train station. It will show a **timetable**. The timetable lists cities, times, and platform numbers. The cities are the different places each train stops. The times show when the trains leave for these stations. Each platform at the station has a number. The numbers show which platform the train leaves from.

You must find a train that goes from this station to Calais. Calais is a French town. It is your next stop. Your train to Calais leaves from platform 3 in ten minutes. Buy your ticket.

Be quick! All aboard!

timetable   list of train stations and times

▼ Travellers gather around the timetable board. They look for information about their trains. The numbers give the train times and platform numbers.

What will you find in Calais?

Task 3: A smaller town

Now, you need to find where two streets meet!

You have been on the train for one-and-a-half hours. Your train ride has come to a station. Now, you are in the French town of Calais. It is not as big as Paris. You have a map of Calais.

When you come out of the train station, walk to the nearest corner. Look for the names of both streets. One street is *Avenue Du President Wilson*. The other street is *Boulevard Jacquard*. Find both of these streets on your map of Calais. Follow the streets on the map until they **intersect** or meet. This is the corner where you are standing. You will start the next part of your journey from here.

*Calais is an important city for ▶ travellers. Many **ferries** (boats) dock and depart between Calais and England.*

ferry	boat or ship that carries people and cars
intersect	when two or more things meet or cross
scale	guide on a map used to measure how far apart things are in real life

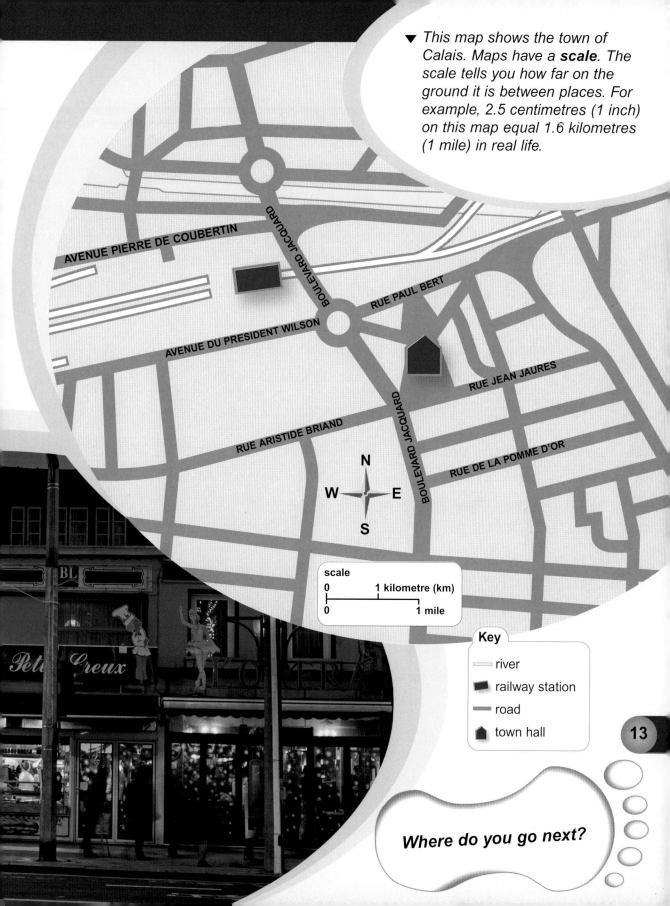

▼ *This map shows the town of Calais. Maps have a **scale**. The scale tells you how far on the ground it is between places. For example, 2.5 centimetres (1 inch) on this map equal 1.6 kilometres (1 mile) in real life.*

AVENUE PIERRE DE COUBERTIN

BOULEVARD JACQUARD

RUE PAUL BERT

AVENUE DU PRESIDENT WILSON

RUE JEAN JAURES

RUE ARISTIDE BRIAND

BOULEVARD JACQUARD

RUE DE LA POMME D'OR

N
W E
S

scale
0 — 1 kilometre (km)
0 — 1 mile

Key
— river
▬ railway station
— road
⌂ town hall

Where do you go next?

Wind directions

Next you need to walk east.

But which way is east? You need to find which way is east. You could use your **compass**. Or, you could find a **weather vane**.

A weather vane is a weather tool. It sits on top of a building. An arrow turns and shows the direction the wind is coming from. On a weather vane, you also see the **cardinal directions**. These directions are north, south, east, and west. These directions guide people. They show people which way to go.

How to tell the position of directions

The cardinal directions are always in the same position (place) on a compass or a weather vane. They are always, clockwise from the top, north, east, south, and west.

cardinal directions   four points of north, south, east, and west
weather vane   weather tool that shows the direction from which the wind blows

Pace it out

You need to walk 4.8 kilometres (3 miles) east. Get out your ruler!

You should go east. Now, you need to walk 4.8 kilometres (km) in that direction. How do you know when you have walked 4.8 km?

Learn your pace

Your **pace** is the length of each right-left step you take. Your pace can help you **estimate** or guess distances.

Put your left foot down. Mark where your heel is. Now, walk two steps—right, then left. Mark where your left toe is. Get out your ruler. Measure this distance. This is your pace. How many feet long is it?

Now, figure out how many paces you walk in 1.6 kilometres (1 mile). 1.6 km are 1,609 metres (5,280 feet). Divide 1,609 metres by your pace measurement. This is how many paces it will take you to walk 1.6 km. For example, if your pace is 0.61 metres (2 feet). Divide 1,609 by 0.61 (or 5,280 by 2). The answer is about 2,640 paces to walk 1.6 kilometres.

estimate   to make a guess about an amount
pace   length of each right-left step (two steps)

Task 4: Heading north

Start walking north.

Now, you have walked for 4.8 kilometres (3 miles). You need to head north. A nearby tree can help you find which way is north. Look at the tree trunk. Do you see green **moss** growing on one side?

Moss likes cool, shady, and **humid** (moist) places. The north side of a tree is more humid than the south side. This is because the sun shines more directly on the south side. The heat from the sun dries up the moisture on the south side. The north side of a tree is not usually in direct sunlight.

However, in southern countries such as Australia, moss grows on the south side of a tree. This is because in the south, the sun shines more directly on the north side.

The mossy side of this ▶ tree will show you which way is north.

humid   moist
moss   tiny green plants that grow in clumps on rocks, trees, and moist ground

20

See the line through the watch? It points to north and south.

Use the sun

Keep walking north, until you reach the beach.

You have been walking north for a very long time.
You think you may be walking the wrong way.

Your watch can help you find north and south. You need
a watch with moving hands. A **digital watch** with only
numbers and no hands will not work. Look at the small
hand on the watch. Move your arm so that the small hand
on the watch points to the Sun. Do not look directly at the
Sun, though! Keep your arm steady.

Now, find the spot on the watch that is halfway between
the small hand and the number 12 (see diagram). Imagine
a line from the middle of your watch going through this
spot towards the Sun. This imaginary line is pointing south.
Continue the line from the middle going in the opposite
direction. This imaginary line is pointing north. Now you
can be sure you are walking in the right direction!

*Have you found
the beach yet?*

digital watch   watch that has only
numbers, not moving hands

Task 5: Get out your compass

Walk on the beach in a northeast direction.

You made it! You have arrived at the beach. Now, you need to walk northeast. You have found your **compass**. A compass has a needle. The needle seems to move. Actually, the needle always points in the same direction: north. You should turn your compass so that its north label (N) matches up with the direction the needle is pointing.

You need to walk northeast. Northeast is the direction between north and east. Start to walk in that direction!

After a few minutes, you are almost at the end of your trip. The special building you have set off to find is nearly in sight.

Other points on the compass

Some other points on a compass are southeast, southwest, and northwest. These points are between the four main directions. For example, southeast is halfway between south and east.

▼ The needle in the compass is pulled, or attracted, to Earth's magnetic north pole. The magnetic north pole is not the same as the North Pole. It is very close, though.

You are nearly there!

Better together

Can you find the lighthouse?

Try using your map and your **compass** together.

A map has a drawing that looks like a compass. This drawing is called the **compass rose**. Place your compass on the compass rose. Now, turn your map and the compass together. The north label on the **compass rose** matches the north label and needle on your compass.

The lighthouse is in a northeast position. A ruler will help you make a straight northeast line. Remove the compass from the map. Keep your map still. Then, put the ruler on the compass rose. Make sure it is lined up with the northeast direction. Draw a line on the map, following the ruler. Follow the line northeast.

Do you see the lighthouse?

A compass rose is an ▶ important part of a map. It shows if places are north, south, east, or west of each other.

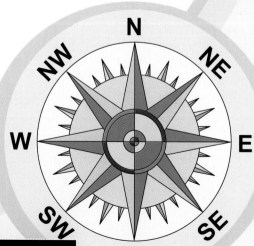

24

compass rose drawing on a map of the directions north, south, east, and west

▼ A compass and a compass rose work together. They tell the map reader which way to go.

25

Have you reached the lighthouse?

Well done!

You have made it to your final **destination**!

You have reached your final destination (place). It is the lighthouse at Calais. It is a very special place.

Lighthouses are tall buildings. They have a huge light at the top. Lighthouses were built to warn ships of danger. Their lights are **navigational tools**. A **compass** is also a navigational tool. A navigational tool helps to guide you. By following the light, ships know which direction to go. Lighthouses also warn sailors of rocks hidden in the water.

Through the fog

Sometimes fog can hide the shore and the lighthouse. Then, even the light will not help. Many lighthouses have foghorns. The horns make a very loud warning sound. This sound helps boats find the shore.

destination   final place, last stop after a trip
navigational tool   tool that helps navigate, or guide, you

You have to climb more ▼ than 200 steps to reach the top. The walk is worth it. The view is beautiful.

27

Finding your way – the modern way

Your trip from Paris to the Calais Lighthouse was not easy. But you made it! You were able to find your way without any modern tools. You used a map, a **compass**, and a ruler. You also used your own knowledge.

A modern tool people use today is **GPS**. These letters stand for "global positioning system". Many cars come with a GPS system.

This person has a ▶ GPS tool in their car. It helps the driver know where he or she is. GPS also gives you directions to places.

GPS global positioning system; tool that uses satellites to help find location
satellite object in space that travels around Earth

A GPS collects information from **satellites**. A satellite is an object in space that travels around Earth. Satellites send back radio signals to Earth. The GPS turns these radio signals into numbers. These numbers show people how far north or south they are in the world. It also shows how far east and west they are in the world.

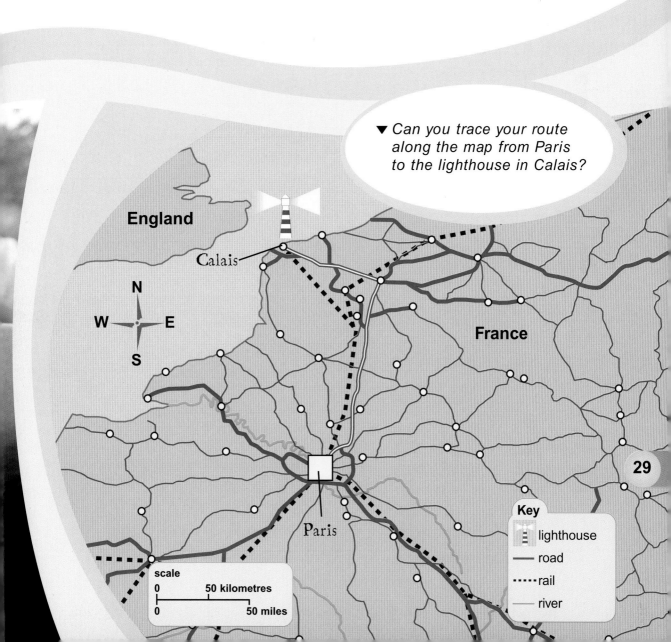

▼ *Can you trace your route along the map from Paris to the lighthouse in Calais?*

England

Calais

N
W — E
S

France

Paris

29

Key

🗼 lighthouse
— road
····· rail
— river

scale
0   50 kilometres
0   50 miles

Glossary

cardinal directions four points of north, south, east, and west

compass tool to help you find the directions north, south, east, and west

compass rose drawing on a map of the directions north, south, east, and west

continent one of the seven largest pieces of land on Earth

destination final place, last stop after a trip

digital watch watch that has only numbers, not moving hands

estimate to make a guess about an amount

ferry boat or ship that carries people and cars. More than one are called ferries.

GPS global positioning system; tool that uses satellites to help find location

humid moist

intersect when two or more things meet or cross

landform feature of the land such as a mountain, river, or beach

map key part of a map where map symbols are explained

metro tube train that runs under the ground

metro line path that a metro train follows

moss tiny green plants that grow in clumps on rocks, trees, and moist ground

navigational tool tool that helps navigate, or guide, you

pace length of each right-left step (two steps)

satellite object in space that travels around Earth

scale guide on a map used to measure how far apart things are in real life

symbol picture that stands for something else

timetable list of train stations and times

weather vane weather tool that shows the direction from which the wind blows

Want to know more?

Books to read

- *Train Journey,* by Deborah Chancellor (Franklin Watts, 2005)
- *Maps and Plans,* by Pam Robson (Franklin Watts, 2003)

Websites

- Go on a city tour and learn about maps at this website. www.bbc.co.uk/schools/twocities/
- Have fun learning mapping skills at mapzone.ordnancesurvey.co.uk/

Learn about maps and explore the world in *X Marks the Spot*.

Be a storm tracker and track a hurricane from start to finish in *Storm Tracker*.

Index

beach 22

Calais 10, 12–13, 26

cardinal directions 14

cities 4, 6–10

compass 4, 14, 22, 23, 24, 25, 26, 28

compass rose 24, 25

continents 4

destination 26

digital watch 21

Eiffel Tower 6, 7, 8

estimating distances 16

ferries 12

foghorns 26

GPS (global positioning system) 28–29

landforms 4

lighthouses 26–27

magnetic north pole 23

map key 8

map symbols 8

maps 4, 6, 7, 8, 9, 12, 13, 24, 28, 29

metro lines 8, 9

metro stations 8–9

moss 18, 19

navigational tools 26

paces 16, 17

Paris 6–10

radio signals 29

ruler 16, 24, 28

satellites 28, 29

scale 12, 13

street intersections 12

timetables 10, 11

tourists 7

towns 4, 12–13

trains 8, 9, 10, 11

trees 18, 19

tube trains 8, 9

weather vane 14, 15